Fractals of Stardust

Lauren Ashley Zamora

BookLeaf Publishing

India | USA | UK

Presentation by *BookLeaf Publishing*

Web: www.bookleafpub.com

E-mail: info@bookleafpub.com

ISBN: 9789360942748

First edition 2024

The Sea of Should

The word should has always shaped me
Promising a path of acceptance
Placating negativity with a shroud of
agreeableness
Who can I be for you today?

When your every day is seemingly filled with an
ocean of uncertainty
Your body begins to crave control more than
food
More than air
As a constant reminder that you cannot swim

Not a harmful dictatorship or a manipulative
robbery
The want to know and not be caught off-guard
The fear of being hurt without notice
To be misunderstood when testing the waters
with your true self

Who built this cobblestone pathway of which I
must go to be happy?
Is life so mundane that the markers of success
are predetermined?
Silent questions, unanswered wonders

Moments of escape, as I trudged forward,
convinced I had just not worked hard enough.

So I walked and walked with each step getting
faster
Walking evolved into running, just to keep
pushing ahead
When suddenly, the path met the edge of a cliff
And then it began to rain

In disbelief, I looked to the sky
Water kissing my cheeks with abandon
My heart cried out for a non-existent promised
land
Tears and rain drops melding into one

On my knees I broke and broke again
The storm growing fiercer, a flood filling the
chasm ahead
I screamed for a reckoning
As the water touched my legs, boiling over onto
land

Panic overturned my rage
As I took a deep breath and stood
Realizing this destination was of my own
choosing
I began to float in the Sea of Should

Coda

This chair may as well be a part of me
For all the time we spend together
Each day, we sit as the world shifts
Upon my porch, my four legged friend and I

No one tells you how quiet life grows with age
How the everyday bustle of living
Becomes muted as you turn into a spectator
Everyone expecting less of you, while you need
more of them

To combat the needing, I sit
Truly, how much trouble can one get into being
stationary?
After many fulfilling decades of breathless
moments
I find myself solitary but not alone

Always beside me in its rosewood frame
I have the most loyal of companions
A virtuoso like no one has ever known
Who sketches the days for me using only six
colors

You would think us lovers in the way I caress
their body
My fingers gliding over each string
Painting a sky, a heartache, a beautiful love
We have grown calloused skin together, in all
that we have lived

As a gentle breeze brushes against my face
I wonder what kind of sunrise you will show me
today
What scene, from what year, with which major
and minor parts
I both yearn for and detest these versions of me

Before the world went black
Every last moment taken for granted
A normalcy that would exist no more
How many years has it been since my eyes went
dark?

Let's not wallow today, you say
Remember that summer when you met
Lost under a tree in a field of wild flowers
And as my heart remembers, my fingers start to
play

Before the Knowing

Climbing a darkened stairway
A small girl is wrapped with anticipation
For in her tiny hands lies her heart
In the shape of a basketball keychain

Smiling to herself in an almost giggle
Step by step by step
She imagines the moment she delivers her gift
How beside himself with joy he will be

They do not have a lot in common
She being barely five and he being an adult
But this will surely bring them closer
And to that idea she is greatly pleased

At the top of the stairs
Sunlight peaks in through covered windows
All the inhabitants of this floor are away
So she quietly makes her way to their room

The door is slightly ajar
With the sun prying its way through the darkness
He is sitting upon a mattress watching television
She summons up her courage and goes to him

It is a fragile yet immovable thing
The relationship between a daughter and a father
How he lays the foundation for her life
Each brick, a standard for those that come after

But what if the bricks are made of glass
That leave her vulnerable to be easily broken
and seen
What if there are no bricks for her to walk on
So she braves the elements of worldly storms
unarmed

Those girls, that girl, this girl
Is for another story

As she holds out her hands
She presents to him, her treasure
He smiles gently as he takes it, brick placed
And for her, it is everything that could be

Overflowing with pride that she got it right
She would remember this moment for years to
come
A time before the knowing
When a simple smile was enough

Forest King

With the awakening sun guiding his way
I follow his tiny pitter patter
Ears and tail on alert
As we go to our silent sanctuary

Leaves sway on the passing trees
A chirp-filled song is dancing on the breeze
Life unseen surrounding us in this wood
He looks back at me to hurry me along

Capturing every new smell
Relishing in the ones already discovered
He makes his claim on every dandelion
Every trunk that was not his before

I am with the Forest King
Master of my Heart
Catching me in awe, he lets out a small grumble
We have almost arrived

A break in the greenery, two branches touch
Seemingly intertwined to create a small doorway
for us
He marches forward, royalty unphased
I bend to cautiously go through

Small rocks now blanket the floor
The water ahead with lullaby ripples
Crystal shades of gradient blues
Sun and shadows bringing different depths to
life

A large rock serves as his throne
For his highness, wading is beneath him
He sits and my eyes try to gulp in the frame
A deep breath soaks my lungs

We stay like this a while
A girl and a sovereign
Until the city beckons us home
My soul dog and I

Quiet on Set

Silent is the street outside
Much more her language
Such an introverted bookworm

The door reverberates with life behind it
Heart beating louder than the bass of the music
Courage pulls upon the handle and enters

More of a shoebox than a bar
More like sardines than people
Her eyes play I Spy until they land on familiarity

Surrounded by unknown faces
A drink is handed as an invitation
Every spike of anxiety leads to a sip

Sip

Sip

Sip

Exchanging newly topped off cups for rhetoric
Wearing a smile as a suit of armor
Emotions heighten at the speed of light

She dances as if to summon a thunderstorm
Every shot a badge of honor
You belong. Have fun.

As hour long seconds pass
The lights begin to awaken
Her body bursting at the seams to withstand the
curtain call

Take a bow for the audience of none
Leave the props at the door on your way out
End Scene.

Fire Starter

Life is fleeting.
Death coming closer every second that passes.
And yet here we are dancing our little dance
around the fires of endless worries.
Not stopping to awe at its glorious light.
Instead seeing the char and the fumes and the
destruction.
Instead of the warmth and birth of commune to
our lonely souls.
We spend so much time fretting.
Trying to please the shadows.
We forget that they possess none but darkness.
You cannot control whether the darkness will
come to the light.
Whether a shadow will come forward, on its
own,
  to embrace the embers of a human heart.
So faint at the get go but as it is fed it can
become a powerful force.

We can only control ourselves in this life.
We have but only one match.
One flame. One fire.
We should choose to burn so bright that those in
the dark yearn to join us.

Be so brave. So courageous. So triumphant
through our downfalls.
That those who have nothing left but an empty
silhouette.
Are forced to see that they are so much more.
That there is so much more.
And that the more is not impossible to reach.

There will always be an opposer.
There will always be obstacles.
There will always be devastation.
There will always be abandon.

Be the difference.
The change.
The light.

Be not afraid of your own fiery greatness.
And help those around you embrace their own.

The light of a fire can either warm or destroy.
The choice is always your own.

Unwritten

Robes dusting along a darkened hallway
A hooded figure holding a lantern makes his
rounds
Corridor so thin that only one can pass in either
direction
A slight clink of the key hanging from his wrist
echoes

The left and right of his path are identical
Thousands of doorways line the walls barely an
inch between them
Each door with a keyhole wherein a choice can
be seen
Confined are all decisions not yet made

He saunters along in a place called The In
Between

Once a heart decides even before the mind can
register
A light glow will emanate through the door
edges and it is time
Taking their key, the door is locked as an
inscription marks the exterior

A choice is made - one possibility goes dark as
the other becomes reality

For less attentive Keepers, Almosts can escape
and run amok
Fleeing down the darkened path
Could Have Beens will bang upon the doors
hoping to disrupt its inhabitants
Haunting reminders of moments already passed

There will be no Regrets during this shift
Responsible for at least a decade of a lifetime
This Keeper will walk and lock each door when
time
And once all assigned doors have been sealed,
story written
He will pass his key to the next

A shimmer begins to spark behind the door
ahead
Readying his key, he approaches and turns the
lock
"Forgive him" is lightly etched upon the door
The Keeper gently smiles and continues on his
way

Knowledge Scraps

So the countdown begins as time folds and
bends and the elasticity of black and white takes
center stage for its moment in the moonlight.
Seek not life in worlds untrue but continue to
harness a hope to better that which you are in.
Moments fall as you toss each penny into your
existential bucket of clay. Mold me.
Hidden within are variations of failures and
triumphs of selves proud and ashamed.
Leap for mankind or one forward step for
humility.
All for nothing yet this tiniest of somethings
takes the lead.
Stand tall like the grandfather clock with the
liveliest song of her voice in your heart.
Conquer your island as they said you never
would.
Bridge those that have burned echoing truth in
sturdiness.
Excuse forgiveness as it bows.
Now the curtains begin to end its tattered green
to lustrous blue.
Love the master of this charade.
Be not the lonely player so lost amongst the
crowd.

For in this pursuit of life and time of now and never of once and happily where dreams come true, I turned one more year older and this silly scrap is what knowledge gained I share with you.

Had I Known

It must have been the third consecutive night we had spent together that week. We were both exhausted from work. Exhausted from life. There was a building frustration in the air that we both contributed to unintentionally. You, a first time emotional lover. Me, a veteran at heartbreak warfare. You, starting the race. Me, waiting for you at the end.

I remember you gave me a massage. You were tired but it was the only way you felt you could help me and I loved you more for that.

We went through our normal nightly routine and once you turned to get comfortable for the night, I lightly rustled your hair and massaged your head and neck in hopes to gently lull you to sleep. I remember feeling you pull my arm into you and again, I loved you more for that.

Once your breathing slowed, I slipped away and turned to my side of the bed. I know you sleep more comfortably alone and honestly, being with you helped me discover that I do too. Knowing

you were there was enough, I didn't need to be
tangled in you.

And with that, I fell asleep
.

That was our last night together.

Now that the pictures have been deleted and we
are no longer friends,

Now that we have done the break-up ritual of
exchanging eachother' s belongings,

Now that we are no longer a "we" because you
are at one stage in your life and I am on another,

I find myself regretful of one thing;

I didn't know and had I known, I would have
loved you more.

Train Into The Night

The L hums a steel lullaby, wheels singing on
the worn track
Downtown lights dance in the window, in her
mind the scenes play back
His smile as they walked along the street,
shining brighter than the moon
The warmth his touch left on her face that now
grows cold too soon

At each stop she searches the crowds, for the
boy she left behind
Quickly turning to check who is changing cars,
in hopes of him she'd find
The sound of his laughter harmonizes with the
melancholic train
Heart yearning for moments before, when will it
be complete again?

Speeding through the darkened tunnels, station
by station so bright
The distance grows between her love, a day so
full set into lonely night
Standing before the opening doors, deafening
silence walks with her home
So she whispers her wishes to the stars, about
him she recites a poem

White Out

Blank slates resonate opportunity.
Clean and open; almost too pure to touch.
Almost too innocent to gaze upon.
A breath of life waiting to be inhaled.
A gasp of air dancing in its own existence.

Pause.
Rewind.

Remember that sincerity?
When happily ever after was the golden rule.
When broken hearts were a fabled monstrosity.
A time before loneliness took its role as your
shadow.
And the surface of your heart remained smooth
as ice.

Take a few steps back.
Back before this monochrome chore grasped
you.
Before the metronome swayed and screamed
your wasted time.
Time you could have colorized to hang in your
hall of self-worth.
Self-worth that is now in question and about to
be found guilty.

Guilty of simply not being enough.

Sit alongside me, so far from those terrors.
Those nightmarish fiends with their judgmental
eyes.
Force the night to show its light.
For these private moments are what truly belong
to you.
In the silence of yourself.
Where all your secrets dissipate,
evaporate,
and fall anew as forgiveness and faith and hope.

Cleanse yourself of your burdens.
So that you can be clean and open.
Ready for each opportunity that will come.
Because it's never too late to start breathing.
No one can tell you it's too late to live.
Your one and only life, begins and ends with
you.

Once you can overcome your past.
And see through your worst of fears.
Will you then be able to let them all fall away.
And start your canvas anew.

Blank slates resonate opportunity...
Just hit Play and go.

Great Stone Dragon

I lay in my bed as the sunlight starts to kiss the
room
House is quiet still and I do not anticipate the
clamor awakening
Today is the day I come of age and my body
yearns for more time

Securing a dagger on my hip and another beside
my ankle
I put my provisions in a small pouch, including a
lucky stone from my sister
Many nights she spent scouring for a trinket to
ensure my survival

As prepared as I ever will be, I sneak out the
door undiscovered
Going through the meadow, leaving the village
to avoid the traditional sendoff
My mother weeping is not the last memory I
want to have of her

Today I woke up eighteen and so that means I
must meet the dragon
It is a ritual that has always been done, like
breathing air, it just is

Upon returning, no one ever speaks of the peril
they encountered

A single golden token is the only evidence of
success
This is presented to the village elders who verify
its authenticity
Then the village celebrates for three days and
two nights

Such a mysterious and daunting task we are
given
As children we tell stories of what it is we
believe will come
Once older, we battle with our self-made
nightmares

Then like today, we begin an adventure that may
be our last
I quickly remove that thought from my mind as I
follow the dip in the valley
The cave is just ahead, I fill my lungs and exhale
my fear

The mouth of the cave is not as gaping as I had
imagined
Firelit torches sporadically line the walls guiding
the way
I walk until the path concludes and meet a ladder

Made of rope it descends below into an abyss I
cannot see
My ears listen for any hint of a sound but there
is only silence
Here at this crossroads, I must decide to
continue or retreat

Unsheathing my dagger, I plunge into obscurity
The cold immediately creeps along my skin
Heart pounding in my ears, my feet find the
floor

Fingers reaching out to find the walls
I make my way through the only opening
Bending to get through, I crawl until I can stand

Inside a pitch black tunnel, a small light dances
So distant and miniscule, I am unsure if my eyes
deceive me
Quietly, I approach until a circular den emerges

Light peaks through a crack in the rock ceiling
above
It spotlights a pile of shimmering coins ahead
In the center stands an ornate gold mirror

Waiting for a dragon to materialize at any
moment

I cautiously make my way forward, awaiting an
attack
Standing before the pile, I look the dragon in the
face

For All Those Times

With eyes that hold both sun and rain
She taught me that storms will always pass
No matter the amount of tears that are shed
No matter the wreckage left behind

Growing together and sometimes growing apart
I look back and know how painfully yet truly I
was loved
Though it was not always clear and easy
Though it was always the best and most

Raising her pride and sunshine
My bold demanding heart would thrust itself
into fires
Only then would I learn that I shine brightly
Only then would I feel the truth when the burn
subsides

How hard I must have made some days
Yet she did what she could without being taught
Always cheering for me even if she was feeling
sad
Always trying to save me from heartache she
already felt

Every year I grow older than she was
Unable to fathom how it was for her then
When it was just us but we made it
When it was just her and she stayed

The folly of children is the thought that parents
are all-encompassing
Built to always knows better, to always be better,
to always do better
Now as an adult I see my mother as a person
Now as an adult I see my mother as my friend

When life was hard and confusing for me
It could only also have been hard and confusing
for her
That thought alone fills my heart with gratitude
That thought alone fills my heart with love

My mother is a force to be reckoned with
A formidable presence in every life she touches
And so I thank you mom for being you
And so I thank you mom for always loving us

Other Side

On the days you wake up on the wrong side of
the bed
When you've already taken two bites before
seeing mold on the bread
When during a test your only pencil runs out of
lead
When your boss picks another for that
promotion instead

During the moments in life when you can't get
things right
When you lose your passport the day of the
flight
When your favorite jeans are two sizes too tight
When you drop your keys in the dark and can't
find a light

In those times when you just can't catch a break
When the best of your friends turns out to be
fake
When instead of a party you are attending a
wake
When you are always the give and they are the
take

Take a look at the world from a different lens
Where you are never alone and have at least one
good friend
Where you are alive with more birthdays to
spend
Where you have things to give instead of to fend

Light a candle and see through the haze
Where you can still travel just delayed a few
days
Where your smile results in your partner's loving
gaze
Where you hid a spare key for the "just in case"

Instead be thankful, do your best to push through
Where you are not starving and two bites are too
few
Where a stranger or teacher helps out of the blue
Where more time with your loved ones is a
better view

You can always be unhappy if determined
enough
Happiness is hard and the choice can be tough
I hope now you see the end can also begin
You don't always have to lose and don't always
have to win

Love Me Still

Today is a perfect day
Sun in the sky, beautiful flowers in bloom
Laughter dancing in the wind
Smiles brighten our faces

Walking through the park
Leash to our soul dog in one hand
Fingers intertwined in the other
We are happy

On days like today
Loving me easy
I hope you love me still tomorrow

Tomorrow when my world is heavy
The waves of fight or flight trying to pull me
under
Lying in bed for hours unending
Under every blanket in hopes to disappear

Shame the reflection in the mirror
A bloody battlefield within my mind
Unsaid criticisms screaming their war cries
Will I survive and return?

On days like tomorrow
When loving me is hard
I hope you love me still

Literary Fugitive

Cursor flashes on an empty page
Waiting an eternity for a deity of creativity to
strike
Fingers dance along the keys
Tracing letters to urge words to materialize
Yet only hovering expectations can be found

Worlds of almost existences
Tangible vivid emotions
Characters of both reality and fiction
Appear and then vanish within a vertical second
Universes abolished by a backspace

A letter emerges grasping to tie itself to another
Deleted and replaced, until a victor finally
prevails
One winner, one breathe, one life
Weaving into words, a rhythmic tapping begins
The melodious escape from a cube shaped
prison

IVX

Back pressed on a newly closed door
The silence engulfs me
Echoing louder than voices and songs

I take a step forward and look at what remains
Scattered bits of love and laughter
Cups and cards and shuffled chairs

The memory of faces that time has molded
But never changed
Kids into adults who together are always kids

How fascinating it is
To be with those who have grown
With the different versions of you

The heartbroken, the enamored
The drunken, the ecstatic
The unsure, the excellent

You can be whoever you are
And they may teasingly never let you forget
But here they are still

I always miss them as soon as they leave

Pieces of my heart in human form
My chosen family

It may be days or months until the next time
Taking comfort that there will be a next time
I crawl into bed and save cleaning for tomorrow

Whozits and Whatzits

Orange mild packets, one spicy hot red
A 9 volt battery that may now be dead
Pair of chopsticks from a takeout order of pho
Neon green lighter and a sparkler from three
Fourths ago

Empty charge cards from the local arcade
Various art supplies from past projects made
Box of rainbow dust to add magic to fire
Instruction manual for a regifted air fryer

Yellow shoelaces still wrapped and unused
A very old rusted blue screw in fuse
Orange chip clip next to a wooden clothespin
Bingo lottery ticket unscratched and could win

Empty superglue bottle with a permanent red
cap
Restaurant menus collected and stacked
Rubber bands and erasers of every color and size
Saved L shaped screwdrivers, a coupon for free
fries

A universal treasure trove each household
contains

Where things once thought needed are stored
and remain
Until the day, they are sought for and retrieved
Is it really junk when it is exactly what you
need?

Star Wishes

Dear Little Explorer
Making wishes to the sky
Watching the world through a window
Hoping dreams will make you fly

Hold on to the magic in your moments
The beauty when alone and in the sun
The sounds of humming in the kitchen
The sour taste of a love potion when it's done

Do not let your achievements grow heavy
And taper down your wings
Do not let the harshness of others and self
Stop you from wanting to sing

Outside there is such a vastness
Compared to your reality so far
You may always feel aside
But do not forget, you are a star

Upon you others may make a wish
Do not diminish making it come true
You must protect your light
Stars have wishes too

There is no perfect ending
As time heals you, you will shine
Your adventures have just begun
Your story and mine